Who Was
Babe Ruth?

Who Was
Babe Ruth?

By Joan Holub
Illustrated by Ted Hammond

Grosset & Dunlap
An Imprint of Penguin Group (USA) Inc.

For Jane O'Connor—JH
For Stephanie and Jason—TH

GROSSET & DUNLAP
Published by the Penguin Group
Penguin Group (USA) Inc., 375 Hudson Street, New York, New York 10014, USA
Penguin Group (Canada), 90 Eglinton Avenue East, Suite 700,
Toronto, Ontario M4P 2Y3, Canada (a division of Pearson Penguin Canada Inc.)
Penguin Books Ltd., 80 Strand, London WC2R 0RL, England
Penguin Group Ireland, 25 St. Stephen's Green, Dublin 2, Ireland
(a division of Penguin Books Ltd.)
Penguin Group (Australia), 250 Camberwell Road, Camberwell, Victoria 3124, Australia
(a division of Pearson Australia Group Pty. Ltd.)
Penguin Books India Pvt. Ltd., 11 Community Centre,
Panchsheel Park, New Delhi—110 017, India
Penguin Group (NZ), 67 Apollo Drive, Rosedale, Auckland 0632, New Zealand
(a division of Pearson New Zealand Ltd.)
Penguin Books (South Africa) (Pty.) Ltd., 24 Sturdee Avenue,
Rosebank, Johannesburg 2196, South Africa

Penguin Books Ltd., Registered Offices:
80 Strand, London WC2R 0RL, England

Text copyright © 2012 by Joan Holub. Interior illustrations copyright © 2012 by Ted Hammond. Cover illustration copyright © 2012 by Nancy Harrison. All rights reserved. Published by Grosset & Dunlap, a division of Penguin Young Readers Group, 345 Hudson Street, New York, New York 10014. GROSSET & DUNLAP is a trademark of Penguin Group (USA) Inc. Printed in the U.S.A.

Library of Congress Control Number: 2011014640

ISBN 978-0-448-45586-0   10 9

Contents

Who Was
Babe Ruth?

He was the king of baseball in the 1920s and '30s. In fact, he broke almost every batting record in the game! But hitting home runs—*lots* of home runs—made him famous around the world.

His real name was George Herman Ruth. His family called him Little George. His fans had other names for him. The Sultan of Swat. The Big Bam. But his most famous nickname—the one that stuck—was Babe.

The way Babe hit the ball was different and

exciting. He swung with all his might and undercut it, popping the ball high and long. Fans crowded into ballparks wherever he went, hoping to see him hit another homer. He tried not to disappoint them.

Babe did everything in a big way. He took crazy chances stealing bases. He argued with umpires. He was loud and always said what he thought. Sometimes that got him into trouble—and into the newspapers.

He didn't look like a superstar athlete. He had skinny legs, small feet, and was often overweight. And he didn't take good care of his health. He ate too much and liked to party. He bought fancy cars and drove too fast. He had amazing energy. He stayed up late—sometimes all night. Then he would play ball the next day. Somehow he'd still hit homers. But sometimes he was just too tired.

Babe's teammates said he would give you the shirt off his back. That means he was really generous. He was also great to fans, especially kids. He signed more autographs than just about any player in history. He loved baseball, and fans loved him.

There have been other great baseball players before and after him, but Babe Ruth was one of a kind.

Chapter 1
Running Wild

Babe Ruth was a wild little boy, always in trouble. There were many boys like him in his rough Baltimore, Maryland, neighborhood. And they all loved baseball. It was the most popular sport in America in those days.

He was born on February 6, 1895. His real name was the same as his father's: George Herman Ruth. His family was poor, same as everyone else they knew. They lived in a noisy, dirty part of town. It was called Pigtown because pigs were brought in on trains and then herded through the streets to the slaughterhouse.

His father, Big George, owned a bar. His mother, Kate, took care of the family. Babe was the oldest of eight children. They all lived in a small apartment above the bar. Poor families couldn't afford good food or good care when they were sick. Many children died young. Only Babe and his little sister Mamie lived to adulthood.

By age six, Babe was always on the lookout for something exciting to do. He hated school, so he wouldn't go. Instead he played in the busy cobblestone streets with his friends. In Pigtown, there was lots of mischief for a boy to get into.

He and his pals stole apples from fruit stands. They played baseball in the middle of the streets or in vacant lots. Wagon drivers smacked their legs with whips and yelled at them to get out of the road. The boys fired rotten eggs back.

The boys called policemen "coppers" since their badges were made of copper. Coppers were Babe's enemies because they were always trying to make him behave and go to school.

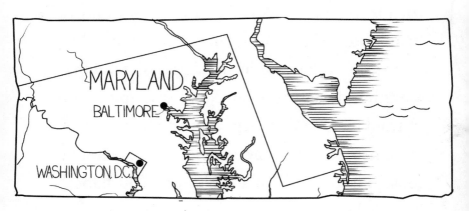

Baltimore was a major seaport. Ships came and went, sailing off into the Atlantic Ocean. Dock workers and sailors hung out on the streets. These were rowdy men who cursed. Babe learned to curse from them. When he should have been learning to read and write, he was chewing tobacco and smoking. He even snitched drinks of whiskey now and then from his father's bar.

He wasn't really a bad boy. He had a good heart and was generous right from the start. But he didn't think things through. Once he stole a dollar from his dad to buy ice cream for all of his friends. Big George spanked him. Just to prove he hadn't learned a lesson, Babe did it again.

He talked back to his parents and wouldn't do anything they said. They couldn't keep him out of trouble. One day they stopped trying.

When Babe was seven years old, his father took him for a ride in a trolley car. Did Babe know where they were going? Maybe not.

Big George took him to St. Mary's Industrial School for Boys and left him there. It was a reform school. A place for troublemakers, runaways, and orphans. There were plenty of schools like this— twenty-nine in Baltimore alone!

St. Mary's was his new home. His family had given him away. This sounds sad, but it turned out to be the best thing for Babe. At school, he would meet someone who would turn his life around. And he would get loads of practice playing baseball.

A BALL'S LIFE

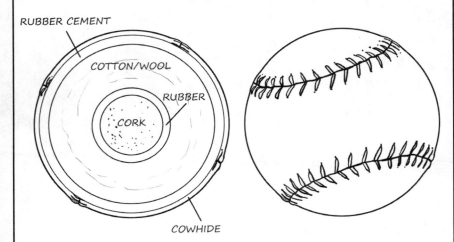

RUBBER CEMENT

COTTON/WOOL

RUBBER

CORK

COWHIDE

A BASEBALL BEGINS AS A SMALL BALL OF CORK. IT IS WRAPPED IN RUBBER, THEN WOUND IN 369 YARDS OF COTTON AND WOOL THREAD. NEXT IT'S COATED IN RUBBER CEMENT, THEN COVERED WITH TWO FIGURE EIGHT–SHAPED PIECES OF COWHIDE. THESE ARE SEWN TOGETHER WITH 108 DOUBLE STITCHES OF RED THREAD. A FINISHED BALL WEIGHS 5 TO 5$\frac{1}{4}$ OUNCES AND MEASURES 9 TO 9$\frac{1}{4}$ INCHES AROUND. IT'S PACKAGED IN PLASTIC WITH A SEAL SIGNED BY THE BASEBALL COMMISSIONER. BEFORE IT'S USED, THE UMPIRE CHECKS TO BE SURE THE SEAL IS UNBROKEN. EACH BALL IS ONLY USED FOR ABOUT SIX PITCHES IN A WORLD SERIES GAME.

Chapter 2
School Days

During his first days at St. Mary's, Babe cried.
He was scared and angry. Everything was different
from home. St. Mary's was a Catholic school.
Babe and the other boys slept in big rooms called
dormitories with their beds set in long, neat rows.

Babe was used to doing what he wanted all day. School seemed like a prison. There was even a locked iron gate at the entrance. A night watchman kept an eye on the boys to be sure they didn't sneak off. Every morning the teachers woke the boys at 6:30. Breakfast was usually oatmeal. For lunch and supper they ate soup and bread. That wasn't much for growing boys! Sundays meant special meals—hot dogs and baloney.

Classes took up most of the day. Babe learned to read, write, and do math. Older boys trained

to become bakers or tailors. After lessons they all played outside in the cement-slab yard. About eight hundred boys lived at the school, and most of them liked baseball. With so many kids around, it was always easy to get a game going.

Sometimes one particular teacher would put on a show for the students with his bat and ball. He was a big, strong guy, about six and a half feet tall. He'd toss up one ball after another and take a hard swing at each one. He'd wallop them high and long across the school yard.

This man was Brother Matthias. He was a good guy and watched over the toughest boys at the school. No one else had ever paid much attention to Babe. But Brother Matthias did. He tried to help him become a good person.

Brother Matthias was calm and firm, but fair with the students. They respected and liked him. When he was around, they behaved.

Matthias started a league with about forty teams made up of the best players at the school. Babe was so good that when he was eight years old, he played with the twelve-year-olds. Matthias let the boys try playing different positions. Babe might have fielded one day, played catcher another, and warmed the bench the next. This was good training.

Babe was an excellent catcher. He was a southpaw, which means he was left-handed. The school only had mitts for right-handed players, so he would catch the ball in his gloved left hand. Then he'd toss the ball up, quickly shake off the glove, catch the ball in his bare left hand, and throw it to the bases.

One day, Babe was catching at home plate. He began making fun of the pitcher. Brother Matthias wanted to teach Babe a lesson. So he told him to try pitching and see if he could do better. Babe hadn't pitched before. Even though he worried he might embarrass himself, he did as he was told.

When he got on the pitcher's mound, Babe felt at home right away. He wound up and threw the ball. Turns out he was a natural. From then on he mostly played pitcher.

If not for Matthias and the other teachers,
there's no telling what might have become of him.
Matthias was like a father. Babe later called him
the greatest man he'd ever known. When Babe
became a famous baseball player, everyone loved
him. But when he was a schoolboy, it seemed that
only Brother Matthias did.

Other boys' families visited them at the school. Babe's parents didn't—even though St. Mary's was only four miles from Baltimore. This made him sad. When he was fifteen, his mother died. A few times over the years Babe went to live at home for a while. It never worked out, and he always wound up back at the school. After twelve years at St. Mary's, he would get his big break and leave for good.

Chapter 3
The Baltimore Orioles

The baseball coach at St. Mary's was outgoing and friendly. One of his friends was Jack Dunn, the owner of the Baltimore Orioles. At that time, the Orioles were a minor-league team.

It was the year 1914. By now, Babe was nineteen and 6' 2". He was a star pitcher on the school team. After watching him pitch in a workout, Dunn offered him $600 a year to play for the Orioles.

Babe was thrilled. And surprised. He didn't realize that pro players got paid. He thought they just played for the fun of it. At St. Mary's, he'd trained to become a tailor. Tailors didn't earn anywhere near $600. He signed Dunn's contract. It was his lucky day!

Along with the rest of the Orioles team, Babe took the train to Fayetteville, North Carolina, for spring training. He'd never been outside Baltimore before. Everything was new to him, including trains. One of the other players showed him how to unfold his bed from the wall. There was a small net pouch hanging on the wall just above his mattress. His teammate told him to rest his pitching arm in the pouch while he was sleeping, so Babe did. The next morning his arm was stiff. The other players laughed like crazy. The pouch

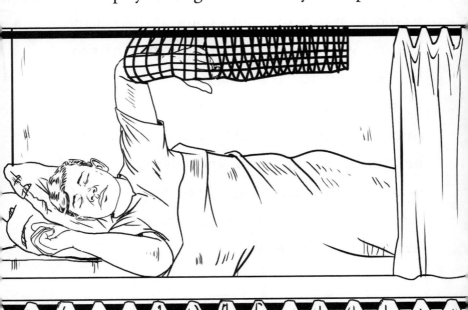

was really for storing clothes. It had been a practical joke.

Around this time, he got his famous nickname. His teammates couldn't help grinning over how little he knew about the world. Someone called him Jack Dunn's "new babe."

Everywhere Babe looked, there was something fun to try. He'd never seen an elevator before. He rode the one in the hotel up and down, up and down. He was used to getting up early because of St. Mary's. Before the other players woke, he would go watch the trains come and go at the station. When he rode a bike for the first time, he was as excited as a little kid.

But nothing made Babe happier than the food in the hotel restaurant. He couldn't believe that he could eat whatever he wanted and the Orioles would pay. At his first breakfast he gobbled down three stacks of pancakes while his teammates watched in amazement.

They were even more amazed when they saw what he did at bat. On March 7, he walloped a fantastic homer—his very first as a pro player. It streaked over the right fielder's head and didn't stop until it rolled into a cornfield. Back then, no one kept distance records. But fans measured it at six hundred feet. That was the longest slam ever in the park.

Soon the Orioles were back in Baltimore for the start of the season. Babe got his first paycheck. One hundred dollars! It seemed like a fortune.

Right away, he bought a motorcycle and zoomed to St. Mary's to take his old school friends for rides. It must have felt great to show them all how well he was doing. Jack Dunn worried he might crash his new toy and tried to make Babe get rid of it. But he wouldn't.

On April 22, Babe pitched his first regular season game. The Orioles won in a 6–0 shutout against Buffalo. He kept pitching that season, winning some and losing some. Nobody had any idea how famous he would soon become. Not even Babe. Still, he was full of confidence.

TAKE ME OUT TO THE BALL GAME

IN 1903, JACK NORWORTH AND ALBERT VON TILZER WROTE THE SONG, "TAKE ME OUT TO THE BALL GAME." TODAY, IT'S SUNG DURING THE SEVENTH-INNING STRETCH, WHEN FANS AND PLAYERS TAKE A SHORT BREAK TO "STRETCH" THEIR MUSCLES. WHEN THE TWO MEN WROTE THE SONG, THEY HAD NEVER EVEN SEEN A BASEBALL GAME!

In June, the Orioles won thirteen games in a row. Hardly anyone noticed. At one Orioles game, there were only seventeen fans. Right across the street from their ballpark was a new stadium. It was the home of a major-league team called the Terrapins. Baltimore fans went to see those games instead.

Babe was one of the best minor-league rookies—the word for young players just starting out. Jack Dunn worried the Terrapins might steal Babe away. So he tripled his salary to $1,800! But without ticket sales, the Orioles were losing money. Dunn had to sell off some players. The **RED SOX** Boston Red Sox wanted Babe. A deal was struck.

After only six months, Babe had hit the big time—the major leagues!

Chapter 4
The Red Sox

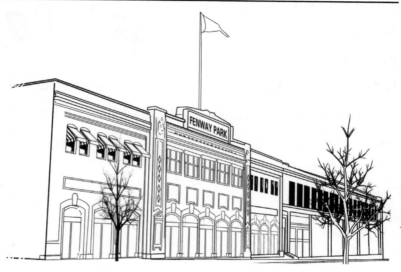

Babe headed for Fenway Park in Boston, home of the Red Sox. Although they'd been world champions in 1912, they were now in sixth place in the American League. He joined the team on July 11, 1914. His first game was against the Naps, a team soon to become the Cleveland Indians.

Right away, the Red Sox manager wanted to see what Babe could do. He told him to take the mound and pitch. Most rookies would have been nervous. After all, this was his first major-league game. But Babe kept his cool. The Red Sox won 4–3.

Babe's teammates expected him to be in awe of them. Instead he treated everyone as his equal. He was always joking around. Other players didn't know what to think about him at first.

No one knew what a great player he would become. In fact, another pitcher on his team was performing better than he was. So in August the Red Sox owner sent Babe to pitch for a minor-league team he owned in Rhode Island called the Providence Grays. Babe missed the Red Sox. He also missed a woman he'd met named Helen Woodford. She was a waitress at a Boston coffee shop where Babe often had breakfast.

After the season ended, Babe married Helen
on October 17, 1914. He was nineteen years old
and she was only seventeen. For a while they lived
in an apartment in Baltimore and were really
happy. But Helen was shy and had no idea what
she was in for. Being the wife of a pro baseball
player like Babe would not be easy.

Babe began the 1915 season playing with the Red Sox again. During his time with the Grays, he'd gotten rid of a bad habit: Without realizing it, he'd always curled his tongue before throwing a curveball. It was a dead giveaway to batters.

Everyone could see the improvement in Babe's pitching. Then, in a game against the Yankees, something historic happened. It was May 6, 1915, and he was up at bat. Another young player might have bunted or hit a grounder, playing it safe. But

Babe swung at the pitch with as much power as he could. *Crack!* The sound echoed through the park. The ball flew. And flew. *Wow!* As it shot up higher and farther, the crowd buzzed with excitement. Eventually it landed high in the grandstand seats. It was his first home run in the majors!

Fans took notice. Who was this new guy? In those days hardly anyone hit the ball superhard. Homers were rare. A power hitter might hit ten in a whole season.

HOW BABE HIT HOMERS

BEFORE BABE RUTH, BATTERS DIDN'T HIT THE BALL AS HARD AS THEY COULD. INSTEAD THEY TRIED TO SEND IT WHERE THEY WANTED IT TO GO. WHEN BABE CAME ALONG, SOME PEOPLE THOUGHT HIS WAY OF HITTING WAS ONLY ABOUT UNCONTROLLED POWER. BUT IT WASN'T. HE STARTED WITH HIS BACK SLIGHTLY TURNED TOWARD THE PITCHER.

HE KEPT HIS EYE ON THE BALL.

THEN HE
TOOK A
LONG STEP.

AND THEN HE
SWUNG AROUND
WITH HIS ENTIRE
BODY WEIGHT.

BABE MADE HOMERS LOOK EASY. FOR HIM,
CONFIDENCE AND TIMING WERE THE MOST
IMPORTANT PARTS OF GETTING A GOOD HIT. HE
WAS THE FIRST PLAYER TO EVER HIT SIXTY HOME
RUNS IN ONE SEASON, AND BACK IN BABE'S TIME,
THERE WERE FEWER GAMES IN A MAJOR-LEAGUE
SEASON THAN THERE ARE NOW.

The Red Sox won the American League pennant that season. They would play the Philadelphia Phillies in the World Series.

Babe could hardly wait to pitch in his first World Series. He loved competition. But except for one pinch hit, he wound up warming the bench. Though the Red Sox won, Babe was disappointed he hadn't played more.

With some of his earnings, he bought a new bar for his father. Sadly, two years later, Big George died in a street fight. Except for his sister Mamie, no one in his family lived to see Babe become famous.

In 1916, the Red Sox made it to the World Series again—this time against the Brooklyn Robins, which later became the Brooklyn Dodgers (and is now the Los Angeles Dodgers). Babe pitched in game two, which stretched into a whopping fourteen innings. The Sox won the series again—and this time Babe played a key part in the championship.

The Red Sox missed out on the league pennant and the series in 1917. But Babe had pitched twenty-four winning games during the season— a career high so far.

Millions of Americans were going to Europe to fight in World War I. The world was changing around Babe, but he didn't pay much attention. His life was baseball.

Chapter 5
Slugger

In 1918, pitchers ruled the game. Batters rarely hit homers. They were happy to even make it to first base. Scoring meant being fast around the bases or quick at stealing them. Because of this, final game scores stayed low, sometimes only a few runs.

Babe was a game changer. He wanted to win by making power hits. However, too much pitching and batting could injure a pitcher's arm. Babe wanted to stop pitching and start hitting. But the Sox manager said no.

With Babe on the pitcher's mound, the Red Sox made it to the World Series again. This time they were playing against the Chicago Cubs. After game three of the series, Babe was horsing around with his teammates. He accidentally punched his left hand—his throwing hand—into a wall. He was supposed to pitch the next day! Babe had really messed up this time.

When he stood on the pitcher's mound in game four, his middle finger was badly swollen. It hurt to grip the ball. Amazingly he still led the Red Sox to the championship. And the Cubs didn't get a hit off of him until the eighth inning.

This meant he pitched 29.66 scoreless innings in a row in the World Series. This was a record that stood for forty-two years.

He'd also hit eleven home runs that year—a big number in those days. Babe knew he was something special. He'd begun with the Red Sox at a salary of $3,500. Now he was up to $7,000. That was a great deal of money in 1918. Still, Babe thought he was worth more. He refused to play the following year unless he got a raise. The Red Sox agreed to pay him one of the highest salaries in baseball—$10,000 a year. Back then, that was enough to buy two or three houses.

Even more than money, Babe wanted the Red Sox to take him off the mound. To make that happen, he had to prove he was more valuable as a hitter than a pitcher. At bat in his first exhibition game in 1919, he did. The New York

Giants pitcher threw, and Babe swung. *Wham!*
He blasted it over the fence. Then he rounded the
bases, reaching home plate in triumph. There are
no official records, but some fans reported that
the ball had sailed an astounding six hundred feet!

Things were looking up. Still, Babe couldn't seem to stay out of trouble. While on tour, the team manager knocked on Babe's hotel room door. It was early in the morning. After a minute, Babe called to him to come in. The manager went over to Babe's bed and yanked the covers down. Just as he'd suspected, Babe was dressed in his street clothes. He had been out partying all night. He had just returned to his room. At the sound of the knock, Babe had jumped into bed and pretended to be asleep.

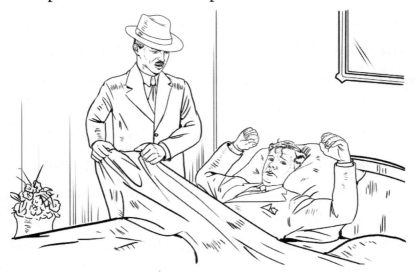

The manager scolded Babe, telling him he needed to change his ways. No one could stay out all night and play ball the next day. Not even a man with Babe's energy.

Over the next few months, Babe behaved himself. He even started leaving notes for the manager reporting what time he came home. Unfortunately he also

went into a batting slump. His record was among the worst in the league. The manager asked him to return to pitching. Babe didn't want to pitch again, but he did.

Then, just as suddenly, he began hitting home runs again. On May 20, he hit the first grand slam of his pro career. A grand slam means he hit a homer with the bases loaded, so four runs were scored. Although the Red Sox didn't make it to the World Series, he set a major-league record with twenty-nine home runs. The national league leader hit only twelve.

Everyone figured Babe Ruth had a great future with the Red Sox. They were wrong.

Chapter 6
The Yankees

In early 1920, the Red Sox sold Babe Ruth to the New York Yankees. The news stunned Boston. Many fans today still think it was one of the worst decisions in baseball history. Babe went on to soar with the Yankees, but the Red Sox didn't win another World Series for eighty-six years.

When Babe joined the Yankees, they had never played in the World Series. They were counting on Babe to make it happen. And they wanted him to hit, not pitch. That suited him fine.

However, things didn't start off well with his new team. He struck out three times in one game and then hurt his ribs swinging his bat too hard.

For weeks, he was more of a strikeout king than a home run king. His first homer with the Yankees didn't come until May after his ribs healed. From then on, he hit home run after home run. He made a notch for each one on his favorite bat.

BLACK SOX SCANDAL

BASEBALL WAS THE MOST POPULAR SPORT IN BABE'S TIME. PLAYERS WERE HEROES. SO IMAGINE HOW UPSET FANS WERE TO HEAR THAT A WORLD SERIES HAD BEEN FIXED. IN THE 1919 WORLD SERIES, IT WAS THE CHICAGO WHITE SOX AGAINST THE CINCINNATI REDS. THE RUMOR WAS THAT SOME WHITE SOX PLAYERS MADE A DEAL WITH GAMBLERS. THESE PLAYERS AGREED TO LOSE THE SERIES ON PURPOSE IN EXCHANGE FOR MONEY. THEN THE GAMBLERS BET BIG MONEY ON THE WHITE SOX LOSING. AFTER THE SCANDAL BROKE, EIGHT WHITE SOX PLAYERS WERE BANNED FROM PROFESSIONAL BASEBALL FOR LIFE. IT WAS A DARK, SAD TIME IN BASEBALL HISTORY.

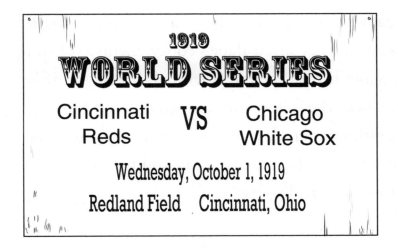

1919
WORLD SERIES

Cincinnati Reds   VS   Chicago White Sox

Wednesday, October 1, 1919
Redland Field . Cincinnati, Ohio

Babe was not only good for the Yankees, he was good for the sport of baseball. Baseball was in trouble because of a terrible scandal. Players on the Chicago White Sox had taken bribes to let the Cincinnati Reds win the 1919 World Series. Ballplayers had always been heroes to kids and grown-ups alike. Fans felt let down and angry.

Babe was the right man to restore fans' faith in baseball. Huge crowds turned out to watch his powerful slugs. By hitting homers, Babe changed the focus of the game. It no longer depended so much on pitching skill. Now batting power won games. Fans liked seeing more action and higher scores. They loved Babe's cocky energy. When he swung his bat, he did it with all his might. If he missed, the follow-through would send him twirling around. It looked a little silly, but Babe didn't care. Because when he did hit the ball—*wowza!* It really flew!

Since there was no TV yet, people listened to games on the radio. Sportscasters described what was happening play by play. They got really excited whenever Babe hit a long one. So did newspaper reporters. They tried to top one another in thinking of nicknames for him like the Sultan of Swat, the King of Crash, the Prince of Pounders, and the Colossus of Clout. It was Babe-o-mania!

On July 19, Babe belted out his thirtieth home run to smash his own record. And he didn't stop there. By season's end he'd hit fifty-four home runs! The National League leader had only hit fifteen.

The Red Sox finished the season in fifth place. They would not win a World Series again until 2004. Many fans thought this was because they'd lost Babe. The Italian word for "babe" is "bambino." The Red Sox's unlucky streak came to be known as the "Curse of the Bambino."

Chapter 7
Good/Bad Babe

Babe didn't look like most other players of his day. They were slender and fast. He was tall and looked top-heavy, with broad shoulders, muscled arms, and a big body atop skinny legs and small feet.

He could really eat. Once, he ate several bags of peanuts, eight hot dogs, an apple, and drank five sodas. Afterward, he got a stomachache. Joking, he blamed it on the apple. He ate big all the time and burped when he felt like it, not caring who heard. Naturally, he gained weight over the years.

News reporters liked him. Because he was so entertaining, they always had something to write about. During a 1928 World Series game against the Cardinals, St. Louis fans booed him after a call they didn't like. Back then, fans would throw lemons, eggs, cabbages, hats, and even umbrellas on the field when they were mad. This time someone threw a soda bottle. Babe picked it up and made a silly show of pretending to throw it back. Fans ducked, but Babe just laughed and tossed the bottle away. The fans laughed with him. The booing ended.

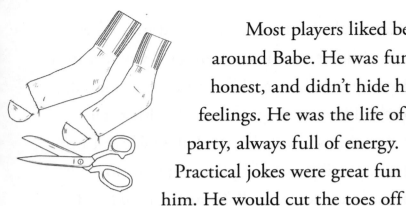

Most players liked being around Babe. He was funny, honest, and didn't hide his feelings. He was the life of the party, always full of energy. Practical jokes were great fun for him. He would cut the toes off other players' socks or nail their shoes to the floor. Babe was very competitive and desperately

wanted to win any game he played, whether it was baseball, shuffleboard, golf, bowling, or cards. But he also encouraged other players and gave them tips to improve.

One player Babe didn't always get along with was Ty Cobb of the Detroit Tigers. Cobb liked the slower style of play that had been popular before Babe. Like many ballplayers back then, Cobb teased players on the other teams. He'd call them names hoping to make them lose their

focus. But when Ty Cobb teased Babe, it hurt his feelings and made him mad.

Games were always during the day. (Night games didn't start until stadiums got electric lighting starting in 1935.) So Babe was free to go to restaurants and parties and have a good time every night. His starting salary with the Yankees was $20,000—double what he'd made with the Red Sox. There were plenty of people around to help him spend his cash and get into trouble.

THE ROARING TWENTIES

BABE CAME ALONG AT AN EXCITING TIME—
THE 1920S. AFTER WORLD WAR I ENDED IN 1918,
EVERYONE WAS FULL OF NEW ENERGY. BEFORE
WORLD WAR I, CARS WERE A LUXURY. BUT DURING
THE 1920S, MILLIONS WERE SOLD. BASEBALL
GAMES AND COMEDY SHOWS WERE POPULAR ON
THE RADIO. SILENT MOVIES WERE
AT THEIR BEST WITH STARS
LIKE CHARLIE CHAPLIN.
"TALKIES" (MOVIES WITH
SOUND) WERE GETTING
STARTED. WOMEN GOT TO
VOTE FOR THE FIRST TIME
IN 1920. THEY STOPPED
WEARING DRESSES TO
THEIR ANKLES AND
WORE SHORT SKIRTS.
HAVING LONG HAIR
SUDDENLY SEEMED
OLD-FASHIONED, AND
MANY WOMEN HAD
THEIR HAIR "BOBBED"
(CUT SHORT). A WILD
NEW DANCE CALLED
THE CHARLESTON WAS

POPULAR. SO WAS JAZZ MUSIC. IF SOMEONE
CALLED YOU "THE CAT'S MEOW" OR "SWELL," IT
MEANT YOU WERE COOL. FOR MANY PEOPLE,
IT WAS A FUN, HAPPY DECADE.

From 1920 to 1933, it was against the law to sell alcohol in the United States. Even so, a famous, rich man like Babe could buy bootleg (illegal) whiskey. He spent many nights gambling, getting drunk, eating, smoking, and joking around with his friends. He was gone so much that his roommate on tour told a reporter he didn't share a room with Babe, he shared it with Babe's suitcase. Babe still made it to his games each day, but often he was tired and not playing his best.

He had a daughter named Dorothy in 1921—
but being a father didn't slow him down.
Sometimes he acted like a big kid himself. He
crashed cars, cursed, and could be rude. He was
also kindhearted and almost always smiling.

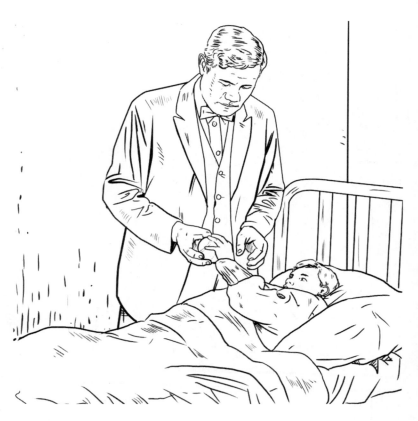

Kids everywhere loved him, and he loved
them. He could be himself around them. He
didn't have to watch his manners, and they
wouldn't try to boss him around. Whenever he
could, he visited children in orphanages and
hospitals. Babe never forgot St. Mary's. He

donated money to the school and paid for the students to come to his games. When part of St. Mary's burned down in a fire, he took the school band on the road with the Yankees. The band played before each game. Afterward they collected money from the crowd to help rebuild their school.

On visits to St. Mary's, Babe would fill his
pockets with coins. He'd toss handfuls in the air
for the boys to chase. Then he would put on a
show for them just as Brother Matthias had once

done. With a swing of his bat, he'd send balls
soaring over the boys' heads. They would rush
to catch fly balls hit by the famous Babe Ruth.

Chapter 8
Superstar

When the 1921 season started, fans were buzzing. Could Babe match his fifty-four homer record of the year before? Many said it was impossible. People took bets on it.

Babe was right where he wanted to be—the center of attention, a star. For him there was nothing more thrilling than slugging a ball out of sight and scoring a home run. He would circle the bases and tip his cap to his fans as they went wild cheering.

Other players studied him closely. They watched the way he stood at the plate and how he swung, trying to figure out Babe's secret. His balance and timing were excellent. He once said that he thought his batting ability was a gift, like a musical talent. One thing was for sure—he made hitting home runs look easy. Pitchers were afraid of him. They tried to foul him out with poor throws. Because if he caught a ball with his bat, watch out!

By the end of the season, he'd proven himself again. He'd beaten his record with an astounding fifty-nine home runs! The other league's best was less than half that at only twenty-three. He was the home run king.

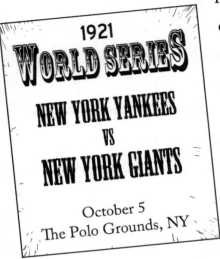

1921
WORLD SERIES

NEW YORK YANKEES
VS
NEW YORK GIANTS

October 5
The Polo Grounds, NY

The Yankees came up against the New York Giants in the 1921 World Series. It would be the best five out of nine games. Going in, the Giants were a strong all-around team. The Yankees depended heavily on Babe, but the Giants pitcher threw outside curveballs. Babe was having trouble hitting them. In game two, Babe slid into third base. Avoiding the tag, he scraped his arm. He scraped it again in the next game. It got badly infected. In game five he hurt his knee. By now,

he felt dizzy and sick. Except for one pinch hit,
he had to sit out the rest of the World Series. The
Yankees lost.

In the 1921 off-season, Babe decided to go
barnstorming. Barnstorming meant playing
games with teams that were not in the majors.
Babe never liked rules and ignored the fact that

barnstorming was illegal for World Series players. He made lots of extra money, but got suspended for the first six weeks of the 1922 season. He spent the weeks off overeating and drinking. For fun, he joined a vaudeville act, singing and telling jokes. And he went into the hospital to have his tonsils removed. By the time he was allowed to rejoin the team, he was out of shape and cranky.

In May he threw dirt in an umpire's eyes and
chased a heckler in the stands. In June he argued
with an umpire and was suspended for five games.
But he was still the star everyone came to see. In
August the biggest baseball crowd ever came to
Michigan's Navin Field. The Yankees were playing

the Detroit Tigers. People without tickets climbed telegraph poles and trees near the stadium so they could watch the game. It was a Yankees win, 11–6.

Somehow Babe still managed to hit thirty-five home runs that year even though he had missed a third of the season. Three other players had hit more. But he stunk in the World Series, making only two hits. The Giants won again.

Afterward, the mayor of New York, as well as his Yankee teammates, told Babe he'd let them down. He was ashamed of himself. He promised

to do better next season. First Babe had to get in shape. During the off-season, he and Helen bought an eighty-acre farm named Home Plate in Sudbury, Massachusetts. The house had twelve rooms and cost a whopping $12,000. At the farm, he kept cattle, pigs, horses, chickens, and a dog named Dixie.

It was a dream come true for a boy who'd grown up poor. He cut back on his eating and quit drinking. For exercise, he chopped wood, ice-skated, hiked, and worked with his animals.

His daughter Dorothy was delighted to have him home. She adored him. He was so much fun, always laughing and joking around. But when the 1923 season rolled around, he left again. She really missed her dad.

Babe began the season in tip-top form. It was an exciting time for the Yankees. Their new home, Yankee Stadium, had just been built. It could hold seventy thousand people. Would fans forgive Babe and fill the seats to watch him?

On opening day, the stands were packed with a reported crowd of 74,200. When Babe came to bat, a pitch sailed over home plate. He slugged it. *Boom!* It was a terrific slam toward right field. Fans leaped to their feet to watch it go . . . and go. Eventually it landed in the stands. Everyone cheered like crazy. Babe Ruth had just hit the first home run ever in Yankee Stadium!

YANKEE STADIUM

YANKEE STADIUM OPENED ON APRIL 18, 1923, IN THE BRONX, NEW YORK. BABE RUTH HIT A TOTAL OF 259 HOMERS THERE, INCLUDING THE FIRST EVER IN THE STADIUM. AFTER THE STADIUM CLOSED IN 2008, A NEW YANKEE STADIUM WAS BUILT NEARBY. TO CELEBRATE OPENING DAY, THE FAMOUS BAT

BABE USED TO HIT
THAT FIRST HOME
RUN WAS BRIEFLY
SET ON HOME PLATE
BEFORE THE FIRST GAME. A BASEBALL SIGNED
BY BABE RUTH IS IN THE STADIUM'S MUSEUM.

After the Yankees beat the Red Sox that day, a sportswriter dubbed the stadium "the house that Ruth built." It was a nickname that stuck.

The season was a great one for Babe and his team. The World Series came down to two rival New York teams—the Yankees and the Giants—for the third year in a row. The past two years the Giants had won. Not this year. Babe was on fire. Instead of letting him hit, the Giants walked him when they could. But Babe still homered in games four and five, and the Yankees took the series. Babe was voted Most Valuable Player (MVP) in the American League. By the end of 1923, he was a bigger superstar than ever.

Chapter 9
Babe-errific!

No matter how famous he got, Babe remained a down-to-earth guy. During the hot summer months, he would buy a cabbage on his way to a game and keep it in a bucket of ice. He'd pull off a leaf now and then and tuck it under his cap to keep cool.

He wasn't impressed by anyone: not by other players and not by presidents or royalty. When he met US President Calvin Coolidge, he called him "Prez." And when he met Queen Wilhelmina of the Netherlands, he said, "Hiya, Queenie!" He called most people "kid" because he had trouble remembering names.

In 1924, Babe had a good year. But 1925 was horrible. Once again he was back to his bad habits. He ate and drank too much and didn't

exercise. By the beginning of the season he had gained fifty pounds and had a potbelly. He broke the team rules by staying out late one night and got suspended and fined. During the season, he fainted and wound up in the hospital for six weeks. It was no wonder that two other players hit more homers than he did that year. He and his wife Helen separated in August. Everything seemed to be falling apart.

Babe knew things had to change. He apologized to his team and then to his fans in a magazine article. During the off-season he began working out at a gym. Soon he was a force on the team again. He set another record in 1926 by doing something that seemed almost impossible. During the World Series, he promised an injured boy in a local hospital that he'd hit a home run for him. He tripled that promise, hitting a record three series home runs! And he wasn't done making history yet.

During 1927 he was
the first player to hit sixty
home runs in one season!
He reached fifty-four homers
the following year, but would
never break his own record.
(When Roger Maris of the
Yankees finally did thirty-four
years later, many Babe Ruth

ROGER MARIS

fans were so brokenhearted that they booed.)

Fans didn't just like Babe. They *loved* him! His
first year playing baseball, he'd gotten only one
fan letter—and that one was from Brother
Matthias. In 1927, he got twenty thousand letters
from fans. Sometimes strangers mailed checks to

him. If he signed and
cashed a check, the
bank would return it
to the fan afterward.
Instant autograph.

Babe signed so many autographs in his lifetime that his signature isn't worth as much as some other players'.

The Yankees became the first team to give players permanent numbers in 1929. Babe was third in the batting order, so he had the number 3. His teammate Lou Gehrig was fourth in the order and got number 4. Lou was a great player, but he was often overshadowed by Babe. The two of them were very different. Lou was calm and quiet. Still, Lou and Babe became good friends.

By now Helen and Babe had been apart for
almost four years. Babe had fallen in love with a
woman named Claire Hodgson. After Helen died
in 1929, he married Claire. Babe, Dorothy,
Claire, and Claire's daughter, Julia, all went to
live in a luxurious New York apartment. Claire
was a no-nonsense wife. She tried to get Babe to
eat right and get enough sleep. Like a mischievous
kid, he found ways around her rules.

In 1930, the Yankees gave Babe a raise to $80,000! This is especially amazing because it came at the beginning of the Great Depression. Although many people were losing their jobs, baseball was king, and Babe was a national hero. He made good things seem possible. If a poor kid like Babe could grow up to be rich and famous, it gave everyone hope.

Chapter 10
Slowing Down

In 1931, two Yankees—Babe and Lou Gehrig—tied for the most home runs, at forty-six each. It was the last time Babe was a league home run leader. Times had changed. Plenty of other players were knocking out forty or more homers a season. Jimmie Foxx of the Philadelphia Athletics hit fifty-eight home runs in 1932, only two short of tying Babe's record. Babe was slowing down, but he wasn't finished making baseball history yet.

One of his most famous homers ever came in the 1932 World Series. It was Babe and the Yankees against the Chicago Cubs at Wrigley Field. When Babe missed a catch playing right field, Cubs fans laughed and booed. He was embarrassed. Next time he got up to bat, he decided to show them.

The first pitch came. It was perfect, but Babe
let it pass on purpose. Grinning, he held up one
finger toward the Cubs stands, counting strike
one. Two more pitches came, both called balls.
Then another perfect pitch. Babe let it pass

again without swinging. He held up two fingers
toward the Cubs fans, counting strike two. They
were going wild. They could hardly wait to see
him strike out.

What happened next is sports legend. Babe made a gesture toward center field with one arm. Was he teasing the pitcher? Or was he calling his shot—planning to send the ball in the direction he was pointing? A third perfect pitch came his way. This time he swung. *Pow!* The ball sailed toward center field and into the stands. A home run! He laughed his way around the bases. Yankees fans were thrilled, but the Cubs were quiet now. Soon the news was everywhere that he'd called his shot. To this day, no one is sure. Still, this was his last series, and he had played it in a big way.

He went on to rack up thirty-four home runs in 1933 and twenty-two in 1934. For a baseball player, he was getting old—almost forty.

In 1934, he went on tour in Tokyo, playing for sellout crowds. Baseball-crazy Japan loved him.

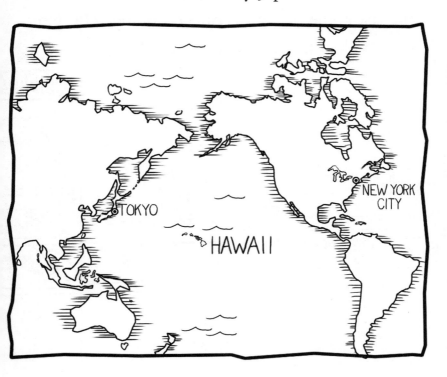

Back in the US, the Yankees
knew Babe was nearing retirement.
They traded him to the Boston
Braves in 1935. He was no longer
the same powerhouse, but he still had star power.
On May 25, he smashed out three home runs
against the Pittsburgh Pirates. The final homer
was the first ever to fly outside the ballpark! The
crowd roared as Babe rounded the bases. This was
the last home run of his career, number 714. No
one else had hit even half that total.

Eight days later, Babe retired from baseball. He dreamed of becoming a team manager. But team owners were afraid to give him the job. Babe had broken too many rules too many times. He kept hoping they'd change their minds. They didn't.

On June 13, 1948, Babe helped celebrate the twenty-fifth anniversary of Yankee Stadium. He was determined to be there even though he was sick with throat cancer. When he walked to home plate, the crowd cheered. They still adored him.

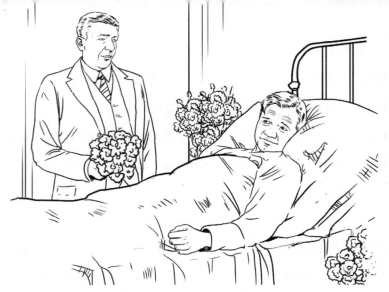

He spent his last days in the hospital, signing autographs and watching baseball on television. He got hundreds of letters from fans. Kids gathered outside, bringing him flowers and pennies. President Harry Truman called to wish him well and the mayor of New York came to visit.

He died on August 16, 1948, at age fifty-three. The flag at Yankee Stadium flew at half-mast.

Later, the Yankees retired his number. No other player on the team will ever wear the number three.

On the day he died, Babe held fifty-four major-league records. He had hit a total of 714 home runs in twenty-two seasons. One out of every four balls he'd hit in the majors had been a homer. His record would not be broken until 1974, by Hank Aaron of the Atlanta Braves. Today he still ranks number three for the most all-time home runs. Only Hank Aaron (755) and Barry Bonds (762) have hit more. Babe was more than a baseball player. He was a legend. He was a hero during tough times when America needed heroes. His big heart and talent changed baseball forever.

There will never be another Babe Ruth.

TIMELINE OF
BABE RUTH'S LIFE

1895 — George Herman Ruth, Jr., is born on February 6 in Baltimore, Maryland

1902 — On June 13, Babe goes to St. Mary's Industrial School for Boys

1910 — Babe's mother dies

1914 — Babe signs with the Baltimore Orioles as a pitcher on February 14
He is traded to the Boston Red Sox
He marries Helen Woodford

1915 — Babe hits his first major-league home run on May 6

1918 — Babe's father dies

1919 — The New York Yankees sign Babe

1920 — Babe hits a record fifty-four home runs in one season

1921 — The Yankees play in their first World Series

1926 — In one World Series game, Babe hits a record three home ru

1927 — Babe hits sixty home runs in one season

1929 — Babe's wife Helen dies
He marries Claire Hodgson

1934 — Babe visits Japan to promote baseball

1935 — Babe hits his last home run in a major-league game
He retires

1936 — Babe Ruth is chosen for the National Baseball Hall of Fame

1948 — Babe Ruth dies on August 16

TIMELINE OF
THE WORLD

The Wright brothers make the first powered airplane flight — **1903**
at Kitty Hawk, North Carolina

An earthquake destroys San Francisco — **1906**

The Boy Scouts of America is formed — **1910**

The *Titanic* hits an iceberg and sinks in the Atlantic Ocean — **1912**

World War I begins in Europe — **1914**

World War I ends — **1918**
A worldwide flu epidemic kills millions of people

The Nineteenth Amendment gives women — **1920**
in the US the right to vote
The Band-Aid is invented

The Baby Ruth candy bar is a hit — **1921**

King Tut's tomb is discovered in Egypt — **1922**

The first Winter Olympics is held in France — **1924**

Charles Lindbergh is the first man to make — **1927**
a solo flight across the Atlantic Ocean

The United States' stock market crashes — **1929**

New York's Empire State Building is finished — **1931**

Franklin Roosevelt is elected president of the US — **1932**

The first Superman comic book is published — **1938**

World War II begins — **1939**
A baseball game is broadcast on TV for the first time

Japan bombs Pearl Harbor — **1941**

World War II ends — **1945**

Jackie Robinson becomes the first black — **1947**
Major League Baseball player

BIBLIOGRAPHY

* Christopher, Matt. **Babe Ruth**. Little, Brown and Company, New York, 2005.

Creamer, Robert W. **Babe: The Legend Comes to Life**. Fireside, New York, 1992.

Gilbert, Brother, C.F.X. **Young Babe Ruth: His Early Life and Baseball Career, from the Memoirs of a Xaverian Brother**. McFarland and Company Inc., North Carolina, 1999.

* Kelley, James. **Baseball**. DK Publishing, New York, 2005.

Montville, Leigh. **The Big Bam: The Life and Times of Babe Ruth**. The Doubleday Broadway Publishing Group, New York, 2006.

Pirone, Dorothy Ruth. **My Dad, The Babe: Growing Up With an American Hero**. Quinlan Press, Boston, 1988.

Ruth, George Herman. **Babe Ruth's Own Book of Baseball**. University of Nebraska Press, New York, 1992.

Ruth, George Herman, with Bob Considine. **The Babe Ruth Story**. Signet, New York, 1992.

* Stewart, Mark, and Mike Kennedy. **Long Ball: The Legend and Lore of the Home Run**. Millbrook Press, Minneapolis, 2006.

* Thomas, Keltie. **How Baseball Works**. Maple Tree Press, Ontario, 2004.

Wagenheim, Kal. **Babe Ruth**. Olmstead Press, Chicago, 2001.

Baseball Almanac. Available at: www.baseball-almanac.com

Major League Baseball. Available at: www.mlb.com

* Books for young readers